Advance ᴸ

"Gillespie captures the lyric beauty of ordinary things. The flamenco steam of a coffee cup dances between reflections of fathers and daughters and waitresses serving up peppermint scented love. Each poem celebrates the simplicity of the superficial while ever so subtly paying tribute to the powerful depth that comes from bearing witness. It's one of those collections I will read again and again."

> — Nancy Murray, author of *One Child for Another*

"*Father of The Red Grotto Used Book Store* is a book populated by fascinating women, a book through which the pronoun she runs like a chant. Doyle-Gillespie's language is tight with potential energy, and when he lets his associative leaps spring--bookbinding to handfasting, a father's bookstore to Masada, marginalia to sunbathing cormorants-- they pull a reader along, gasping."

> — Jennifer Browne, lecturer, Department of English, director, Frostburg University's Frostburg Center for Literary Arts

"You will want to read Ed Doyle-Gillespie's poems out loud. Over and over again. His words are hypnotic. His words are honey-sweet and smooth. Yet there is a rawness to his words, they will make you sweat. My favorites in this collection are "Women in the Half-Moon Cafe" parts One, Two, and

Three. They are interspersed throughout the collection and when each one shows up it feels like seeing a dear friend."

—Alexandra Hewett, author of *Shimmer*

Father of the Red Grotto Used Book Store

Father of the Red Grotto Used Book Store

E. Doyle-Gillespie

Apprentice
House Press
Loyola University Maryland

First Edition

Paperback ISBN: 978-1-62720-502-3
Ebook ISBN: 978-1-62720-503-0

Printed in the United States of America

Managing Editor: Jack Stromberg
Design: Claire Marino
Promotion Plan: Eisa Abu-Sbaih

Published by Apprentice House Press

Apprentice
House Press
Loyola University Maryland

Apprentice House Press
Loyola University Maryland
4501 N. Charles Street
Baltimore, MD 21210
410.617.5265
www.ApprenticeHouse.com
info@ApprenticeHouse.com

Dedicated to Pi, Elaine, Sean, Nancy, Jennifer, Alex, Marla, Cat, and everyone else who helped me find and hone my voice.

Contents

The Art of Protective Spells and Library Science

She finds, finally, that she can fly
these books – each spine title of them –
from the stacks with a blank, unfettered
thought and a heavy dose of Athena magic.
Never leaving the covenstead
of the circulation desk,
she is reading the runes
of the head librarian's tattoo back
when a strap falls from her shoulder.
She is burning parking lot incense
when the clock gives her time to smoke.
She is throat chanting like Mongolian soul
herdsmen deep in the nautilus
of the library's spire.
She is willing pages of text and marginalia
to sunbathe like cormorants come back
from the sea,
to hunch over stacks of hand-worn
broken backs,
and to mantle on the conditioner air currents
when the pyres rise and this town becomes
a second-coming Salem, reborn and risen in ashes.

As When Cities are Built Atop Ruins

She is bookbinding,
like handfasting, with her shorthand
fast filling her mother's margins
of each tattered attic book.
Marking her way,
with words that betray, she makes
opaque the meaning of all of this.
She summer-stays in a used and worn
anthology from the back of the stack,
finds marginalia remains
in her mother's grad-school hand saying
"more lexical difficulty here."
She is bookscribing now
across that which is already inked and worn,
hastily etched in ball point,
scrawled in Flair of manicure-red
"J Campbell – refusal of the quest!"
And she is reading her mother's
ancient screed,
and seeding the corners
with words of her own,
through watermark coffee circles
across the time-worn signature
of a leaking attic.

Conditions of Her Indenture

She isn't like this, actually,
with her talking about liquid modernity,
turning our night into her word palace.
Herding us around the corner
to this place that overflows
with Styrofoam Greek and Chinese steam,
with grease on the checkerboard floor,
explaining more and more
about an uprooted youth.
She uses wounded words
carried in her fractured DNA
from Punjab to Trinidad
to the cold-bone genocide desert
that birthed her a mind
like a never-sated Wendigo.
And this is when she will fold up
the night, actually, saying that
she wrote the best of her words
while it was broad daylight,
while she nursed the overflowing bowls
of udon that they serve in this place,
while construction thundered
in the street just beyond
the restaurant's tinted glass.

Father of The Red Grotto Used Book Store

Farther into your novel,
I recognize myself as the father.
You typed me as the patriarch
who stacks the stocks of the family shop,
who stands too tall
for the small store room ceiling,
who chose to paint a paint too red for
a tribute to the gentrifying neighborhood gods.
Farther into your novel,
he grows as dogeared as I have –
as old men do –
living down dogeared alleys
in dogeared days like these.
He does not share my shaving
of the sugar-and-coffee beard each day,
and he does not chin himself
on the most stalwart of
the basement's pipes.
He does take in tomes
from the students
who feel they have been
betrayed and befuddled by them,
from the wandering jigsaw women
who swear they have learned
enough from them,
from the broken houses
that pour books out like egg yolk.
We, the novel father and I,

both fill the store's scent with
nutmeg and dust until
the book stacks collapse,
and the place is blessed with a glorious tumult.
Farther along in your novel,
when the hodgepodge people have
grown loud enough in his head,
he goes out of the house
as I did one night,
with a paint redder than red,
to dress the door of the family store
and mark where the chosen children live.

After the Reading, She Will Sign Copies

Tonight, straight out of the gate,
there is sriracha in her sweat.
She is at a best-selling book signing,
spice rising in clouds as she asks
each one where they are from,
inscribes a beloved copy,
and drinks the whiskey
that the books sellers have brought
to her as tribute.
There is a twisting tunnel carpel
pain that struggles to thwart her
as she slashes each book
with her signature salutation.
And later, she flounces her t-shirt
in the heat – braless –
and confesses that
her father's bookstore grew
to be the Masada of her childhood.
That is why she wrote him as Esau.
That is why she wrote him as Samson.
That is why she made him swing his books
like the jawbone of an ass.

Morning and the Möbius Unravelling

She loved his hands
for cupping coffee in
the offering Buddha way.
Double-wrapped, calloused,
seeking heat between
double-woven fingers and thumbs.
She would crisscross herself up,
tuck bare feet under cotton thighs
and let him be the raconteur
"for one time more."
He taught her Möbius strip folktales,
and the paradox of killing a grandfather
such as his.
"Pop-pop could die young and slowly"
before he became the razor-strap klansman
"who tossed whiskey in my mother's eyes."
"And I could be both dust and live
at the same time
as I watched him die."
And she sat, morning crisscross,
loving the way his fingers drew infinity
in the air – figure-skater grace –
then returned to cradle-cup
his coffee and take the next drink.

Chimney

A good place to start is a chimney
left alone in the middle of the woods.
It will be drenched in moss,
lost against the verdant chaos,
feigning as though it grows
from the floor of the forest itself.
With a chimney lost so long
in the middle of the woods,
you can ask your questions aloud
for the first time.
Time and time again, it will deny
the broken square of the house
that birthed it.
It is as natural, it will say,
as the split-wood fence
that hides itself in a nearby thicket,
mimicking the trees and the bramble confusion.
It makes the same sense as
the overgrown rails, crossties,
and field-side spikes that hide
in the wild oriental bittersweet.
That chimney will testify that it
grows as wild here
as do the lichen headstones
that grow down the road,
sprouting from the loam,
knowing nothing of the mason's work,
the withered flower tributes,

or the solder-skeleton boys
buried beneath their
monumental feet.

Women in the Half-Moon Cafe Past Dark #1

During your story,
I watched how steam,
again, was becoming a flamenco –
out of your cup –
up and up twisting in coils
like her arms turning *floreo*,
blossoming enough of a wisp
to become her waist and her hips.
You are still seeking the author,
you say, as my steam flamenco dances.
You are finding the stories of journals
in the stories of journals
and his descriptions
of crossfire women
of food and of wine
and long wooden tables
in barricade basements
with the bombs
breaking the frost
all around him.
"He was actually starving
when he wrote this.
The whole country was,"
you almost whispered.
And he walked the country
whole, on broken feet,
on refugee roads,
until he came to a field,

the storied journals said,
where the snow covered
the freshly killed,
and steam rose in grace
like coils of coffee cup flamenco.

Finger Bath

Instead, she used her fingers.
She denied my tribute
of a ragged cloth -
knitted, woven
constellation of holes –
and, instead, curled her hands
into tiny, crescent,
semi-circle claws.
"That can only push soap
around and around
and off of you," she offered,
burying the mantle
once and for all.
Manicured sickles digging
ruts into her skin,
she echoed in my shower
"This is how you get the soap in."
Scarifying herself ruddy,
dissolving a designer bar
of lavender in her palms,
she asked if the cloth was
some trick from my childhood –
a mother's rag of snot, dead skin,
and waste – meant to carry
the last day into the next.
"This way," she said, scratching
furrows into the topsoil
of her body,

"you dig it all away."
You send it down the drain –
sow the soap so deep
into you that when
it is summer,
and you sweat,
the only thing that the heat
will wring out of you
is a cloud of flowers –
the petrichor
of your personal rain.

Gala for the Opening of the Art Nouveau Wing

When you create the context,
make sure she is next to Klimt's Kiss,
and that flat champagne will sustain her
through the marble sarcophagus and the
largess of brittle revenant women.
She is looping two fingers through
the black high-heel sling backs
that she has replaced with bare feet
against the slick stone floor.
She is arching in towards the
gold-leaf pair, undone red hair,
and saying
"This girl is in her rapture, I swear."

Women in the Half-Moon Cafe Past Dark #2

She is in love with the fourth woman
at the counter, because the fourth woman
at the counter is writing the life
of a *jibaro*
in her black and white composition book.
She is eating eggs at midnight,
this fourth woman,
and ignoring the other three as they
battle their Spanglish words
across speckled linoleum.
She is in love,
because the fourth woman is
using her pen
to hew out the farmer's crooked form
between thick-cut bacon, fried eggs, and the green tea
that has sustained her through the all-night
of this diner.
He will be alone in a mountain shack,
mutters the fourth woman,
and its roof will be made of tin.
She listens, she wipes splatters and
she catches fragments,
because the other three
talk with their hands and beat rhythms
like Cuban heels against frosted glass.
The roof is made of tin,
and in the end,
the fourth woman says,

the *jibaro* will walk out
into the jungle,
gather dirt from the grave
that she gave us in the first chapter,
and have him swallow the soil.
That will make a sacrifice of him,
says the fourth woman –
who the midnight waitress
now loves with
all of the rust and peppermint
in her soul –
and that sacrifice
will make the mountain rejoice.

What She Teaches Me About Skin

I asked her, and she told me,
and she showed me,
dishabille from shower to bedroom
to upstairs library,
how she captures her cassolette,
and settles scent behind each ear.
She raised an eyebrow
"expected that you knew,"
how she would anoint herself,
two fingers deep,
she told me, between towels
and the finding of autumn stockings.
Hinting behind each ear
is enough,
on some days, or coaxed up,
on others
like *poi* – generous
and mingled with all five fingers.
This is when it is dense, glistening,
pushed through her hair
to slick it back
when she wears it
cut short like a flapper,
or a pixie, or a boy.
If she must,
she told me,
in the fractured hours,
between bookend showers,

she will cup the musk
of the waning day and
adorn her neck for
the crowded train,
the day-dream commuters,
and the long ride home.

Making Manifest

There is a honey-sugar moon
gloaming over this town
that we have conjured,
and I've decided to believe
in astrology, just for now.
So, I am the mage of a Scorpio coven
that gathers in the ruins
of the old, abandoned mill.
My hex is why your neck does not
retreat from the punishment
of my mouth
– clenching teeth,
sea-salt aperitif.
Libra supplicant at last
paying her penance.
Tonight, I will agree
that haint-haunts stock themselves
to the rafters of your high-gabled house.
They were the scullery maids and slatterns
of this place that died tied
to their cast-iron indenture and
the roving hands of the owner's son.
We will make carnival for one of them
on the bare stone of the kitchen stairs,
spectacle for a disembodied wraith woman
who waits for the toff, still,
behind the pantry door.
I will beg Logic to forgive me,

and give me a one-time pass to swear
and affirm that at least,
one succubus,
this succubus, is solid-real.
See, you will beard as if
the wire-rimmed librarian of this
one-off Brigadoon town of ours,
wings folded, trimmed and tucked
below your second-hand cardigan sweater.
You will lure me and leave me
in the stacks – classics brooding over
my bare-back lacerations – and you
are tying back sugar-honey chaos
as you go to take stock
of what is overdue.

Distraction Portrait

You are naked, and
the art professor has told you
to stand contrapposto so that
we can sketch soleus shaded shadows
of that thick standing leg.
I am brutalist graphite
against the grain of the page,
describing the heft of your breasts,
and the torsion of your turning neck.
You look to your left, just so,
and I imagine you lost in the moment
of a woman's passing redolence –
coffee and eucalyptus.
You turn to see, I envision, that she
is zaftig, and the soft wind, just then,
is pleading with you to please
stand perfectly still
for one moment more.

Blue House Residency

She would follow Frida Kahlo down
stairs like these, midmorning, midsummer,
smoking American Spirit,
drinking chicory cold instead of coffee.
Out behind the bodega,
the boarded-up family center,
the beer distributor,
on concrete steps glistening grey,
just hosed down by the tab-keeper,
she would keep pace with the long-braided
seeker of animal souls and atavism man.
She would take a sip,
and she would ask "Free"
if she will make mosaics today
from the shattered-plate, porcelain alleyway
glass, or if she will stay with paint,
making a deer with a placid Latina face –
pierced like St. Sebastian –
that has broken free across three lanes
of the freeway's hemorrhaging veins.

Women in the Half-Moon Cafe Past Dark #3

She changed her mind,
at the counter that night.
She decided, now,
that she would tell the story
in Tuscany,
and that the man was *Arditi*
in the last war.
It will all take place
at his wedding,
in his head,
dead men burning
behind his closed eyes,
while his guests toast
the lovemaking
that he and the woman will
do forever now.
He will wander on to the patio
while musicians play,
a fiasco in his good hand
while the priest dispenses blessings,
while the wife dances with her brother,
tarantella.

Acknowledgements

I would like to thank Pi, Elaine, Sean, Cat, Marla, Nancy, Alex, and Jennifer for your insight and support. Some of you used your time and talent to read and reread my work and give me feedback. You challenged me to climb to that next wrung. Some of you goaded me to get out of my own head and think about how I was going to introduce my work to the outside world. All of you gave me your care and support. You believed in this project and in me as a writer. Thank you.

About the Author

E Doyle-Gillespie is a writer, poet, and teacher from the Baltimore area. He holds a degree in History from George Washington University, and a Master of Liberal Arts from Johns Hopkins University. He is the author *Gentrifying the Plague House, Aerial Act*, and other books of poety.

Apprentice
House Press
Loyola University Maryland

Apprentice House is the country's only campus-based, student-staffed book publishing company. Directed by professors and industry professionals, it is a nonprofit activity of the Communication Department at Loyola University Maryland.

Using state-of-the-art technology and an experiential learning model of education, Apprentice House publishes books in untraditional ways. This dual responsibility as publishers and educators creates an unprecedented collaborative environment among faculty and students, while teaching tomorrow's editors, designers, and marketers.

Outside of class, progress on book projects is carried forth by the AH Book Publishing Club, a co-curricular campus organization supported by Loyola University Maryland's Office of Student Activities.

Eclectic and provocative, Apprentice House titles intend to entertain as well as spark dialogue on a variety of topics. Financial contributions to sustain the press's work are welcomed. Contributions are tax deductible to the fullest extent allowed by the IRS.

To learn more about Apprentice House books or to obtain submission guidelines, please visit www.apprenticehouse.com.

Apprentice House
Communication Department
Loyola University Maryland
4501 N. Charles Street
Baltimore, MD 21210
Ph: 410-617-5265
info@apprenticehouse.com • www.apprenticehouse.com

Printed in the USA
CPSIA information can be obtained
at www.ICGtesting.com
LVHW021138011123
762299LV00009B/86